21st Century Skills Library

ROAD TO RECOVERY

ELEPHANT SEAL

Susan H. Gray

Cherry Lake Publishing
Ann Arbor, Michigan

Published in the United States of America by Cherry Lake Publishing
Ann Arbor, MI
www.cherrylakepublishing.com

Content Adviser: Dr. Burney Le Boeuf, Department of Biology, University of California
Santa Cruz, Santa Cruz, California

Photo Credits: Page 20, © Ralph A. Clevenger/Corbis

Map by XNR Productions, Inc.

Library of Congress Cataloging-in-Publication Data
Gray, Susan Heinrichs.
  Elephant seal / by Susan H. Gray.
     p. cm.—(Road to recovery)
  ISBN-13: 978-1-60279-038-4 (hardcover)
  ISBN-10: 1-60279-038-8 (hardcover)
  1. Elephant seals. I. Title. II. Series.
  QL737.P64G73 2007
  599.79'4—dc22   2007004447

Cherry Lake Publishing would like to acknowledge the work of
The Partnership for 21st Century Skills.
Please visit www.21stcenturyskills.org for more information.

TABLE OF CONTENTS

CHAPTER ONE

DEEP-SEA DIVERS

A large group of northern elephant seals rests in the California sun.

Hundreds of northern elephant seals are swimming deep in the ocean,

heading to Alaska. One seal comes to the surface and breathes deeply. It

breathes out and goes under again. Down it goes, 300 feet (91 meters).

The water is freezing cold, but the seal keeps going. It dives down 300 feet deeper, and all sunlight disappears. The animal's heart beats once every 10 seconds. Blood vessels in its flippers shrink. This forces more blood to the brain and the core of the elephant seal's body.

An elephant seal rises to the water's surface to breathe.

Elephant seals belong to the group, or family, of earless seals. Scientists call it the phocid family. The seals actually have ears. But they don't have little earflaps on the sides of their heads.

The phocid family includes both the largest and the smallest of all seals. The smallest is the ringed seal. It weighs about 110 pounds (50 kilograms) as an adult. Elephant seals are the largest. They can weigh as much as 45 fully grown ringed seals! Other members of the phocid family are the gray seal, the leopard seal, and the harp seal. What other characteristics do you think scientists use to classify animals?

Deeper and deeper the seal swims into the pitch black. Its stiff whiskers twitch in the ice-cold water.

Time passes—30, 40, then 50 minutes.

Suddenly, something brushes past the seal.

A small shark is making its way in the darkness.

The seal grabs it and swallows it whole. Not a bad snack! Now it is time to head for the surface to take another breath.

CHAPTER TWO

AN ELEPHANT SEAL'S LIFE

An adult elephant seal can weigh thousands of pounds.

Northern elephant seals swim the Pacific Ocean from Baja California

in Mexico up to the Aleutian Islands of Alaska. As adults, males can reach

16.5 feet (5 m) in length and weigh about 5,000 pounds (2,268 kg). That's

The fur coat of the adult elephant seal is dark silvery gray to brown.

the same weight as two cars! Females grow to be about 11 feet (3.4 m) long

and weigh more than 1,300 pounds (590 kg).

Nearly half of the seal's weight can be in its blubber. Blubber is a thick layer of fat just beneath the skin. Blubber helps keep the seals warm during their deep-water dives in cold Pacific waters.

Elephant seals have dark, silvery fur coats. Every year, as the weather warms, the seals shed their fur. This is called molting. During a molt, the fur peels off, taking with it the top layer of skin.

Northern elephant seals are among the greatest travelers of the animal kingdom. They make two round trips each year, starting in California or Mexico and ending in Alaska. In one year, a seal can travel more than 13,000 miles (20,921 kilometers). Scientists think elephant seals take naps as they travel. Some of these naps are probably quite long. The seals can stay underwater for up to two hours!

In the winter, they arrive at the islands near Mexico and California. Males, or bulls, get there first and begin to compete with each other. They

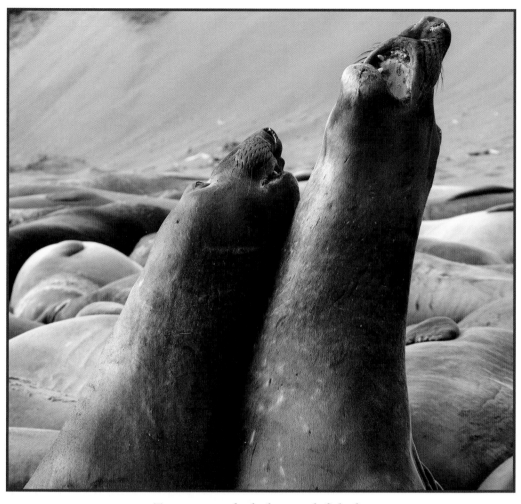

Two young male elephant seals fight for position by bellowing at each other.

make loud snorting, bellowing, and drumlike sounds. They bare their

teeth and lunge at each other, and the bites draw blood. The dominant males are the winners in these contests. They are the ones that will mate with the females.

Soon those females, or cows, arrive. A few days later, they give birth to the baby seals, or pups, that they have been carrying for months. A pup weighs about 85 pounds (39 kg) at birth and has a black coat. It drinks milk from its mother for about a month, tripling its birthweight during that short time.

A young black elephant seal pup lies next to its mother.

Two silver-gray pups play on the shore. Pups must learn to swim, dive, and catch fish and squid to feed themselves.

At about one month, a pup's life changes dramatically. It sheds its black coat and becomes a beautiful silver gray. Its mother abandons it and no longer provides any milk. The pup then begins to practice swimming and diving. While learning these skills, pups lose almost a third of their weight!

It takes pups about two and a half months to learn to swim and dive well. Then they leave to find food on their own as they travel north for the first time.

In the meantime, females mate with the dominant males. Soon after that, all the seals head north. It takes weeks to reach Alaska. Once they arrive, they spend their time swimming, diving, and eating. After four to six weeks, they head south again, swimming back to California and Mexico. After arriving in late spring and early summer, the seals molt, then again move north.

Learning & Innovation Skills

Elephant seals are named for the enormous nose of the male, sometimes called a proboscis. The nose begins to enlarge when the seal is about four to five years old. It is not completely developed until males are fully mature at nine to ten years of age. It grows so long that it can actually reach into the mouth. Can you think of another animal with a proboscis?

CHAPTER THREE

A NEAR DISASTER

Blubber helps keep the elephant seal warm in the cold water.

The elephant seal's blubber is important in keeping the animal alive. It

stores energy for times when the seal is not eating. It keeps the seal warm

during its incredible dives into cold water.

But at one time, blubber was the cause of many seal deaths. Hunters killed thousands of elephant seals just to obtain the animals' fat. Hunting for whales was often dangerous, but not hunting for elephant seals. When the seals came ashore to have pups or to molt, they were easy targets. They were big, clumsy movers. Also, they were unaware of any danger and did not flee from the hunters.

Hunters killed elephant seals by the tens of thousands. Quite often, they killed the seals, trimmed away their fat, and left their bodies to rot on the shore. They sliced the blubber into

Learning & Innovation Skills

During the 1800s, the population of the United States was growing. Many people were moving west to search for gold. Everyone needed oil to light their lamps or to lubricate their machines. Some of the best oil came from whale and seal blubber. How do you think this affected the elephant seal population?

This colony of elephant seals lives at Point Piedras Blancas on the California coast.

smaller pieces, then heated it to produce a high-quality oil. The higher

the demand for oil, the more elephant seals were killed.

Seal colonies began to shrink and disappear. By 1892, the only colony

left was on Guadalupe Island near Baja California. Scientists estimate that at one point, there were fewer than 100 northern elephant seals left on Earth. The animal was nearly extinct.

Northern elephant seals are an important part of the food chain. The food chain is the order of who eats whom in the wild. Elephant seals are carnivores, or meat eaters. They eat sea animals that are smaller than they are. Among their foods are squid, octopus, crabs, eels, fish, skates, rays, and sharks.

Although the seals are huge animals, they are sometimes eaten by other sea creatures. Great white sharks and killer whales feed on them.

Like carnivores that live on land, seals have pointed teeth called canines, or fangs. What other animals do you know that have canines?

Elephant seals spend almost all of their time diving to great depths to avoid the sharks and killer whales that hunt near the surface.

If they escape all attacks, female elephant seals can live to be about 20 years old. Males can live for about 14 years.

The great white shark feeds on elephant seals. It can reach a length of 35 feet (almost 11 m).

CHAPTER FOUR

A BIG TURNAROUND

*In the past, the hunting of elephant seals
drastically reduced their numbers.*

In 1922, government officials in Mexico decided to protect the elephant

seals. That year, they banned all hunting of the animals. They even posted

armed guards to keep watch on Guadalupe Island.

*This sign warns visitors not to disturb the sea animals
at San Simeon Beach State Park in California.*

Not long after that, the U.S. government made it illegal to hunt

elephant seals. Today, it is still against the law to hunt them.

The laws have made a huge difference. Not long after the seals became protected, their numbers began increasing. They also started showing up on other islands. They appeared on islands near Baja California and along the California coast. Every year, groups would come, have their pups, find mates, and molt.

The colonies grew and grew. In time, the seals needed more room. They began to appear on the California mainland. In 1975, the first mainland pup was born.

As elephant seal numbers bounced back, problems arose. In some places, people wanted to get close to the seals or get their attention. Other people would toss rocks at the seals. Some would even send their dogs after them! Now, there is a law that protects the seals from being harassed. It says that people are not allowed within 20 feet (6 m) of the animals.

Life & Career Skills

Early in 2006, California's Marine Mammal Center took in some orphaned elephant seal pups. When the pups were first found on the coast, they were thin and covered with scratches. They stayed at the center and at a local zoo for weeks to fatten up and learn to swim. Their keepers finally released them back into the ocean. Right away, the pups showed what strong swimmers they had become.

The pups were lucky that the Marine Mammal Center was there to help them. The organization, started in 1975, rescues sick and orphaned seals, sea lions, whales, porpoises, dolphins, and sea otters. It helps them recover and return to the ocean. Almost all of the organization's workers are volunteers. Volunteering is a great way to get involved in things that you care about.

Today, scientists try to keep track of the seal numbers. This is quite difficult because not all of the seals are at home at once. Males and females arrive from Alaska during different months, and they leave in different months. Pups are not always with their parents. Sometimes they are off swimming. Nonetheless, scientists see that the colonies have grown every year.

CHAPTER FIVE

ELEPHANT SEALS TODAY

The elephant seal is making a remarkable comeback!

Everyone is amazed at how well the elephant seals have recovered.

However, it took many years and very tough laws for this to happen.

Scientists think there are now more than 150,000 seals. This might be as

many as there were before all the hunting started.

Things have changed, though, since they began to recover. Now, there

are more people living in California and more tourists visiting the area.

New dangers have cropped up.

This photographer must take pictures without
disturbing the elephant seal colony.

Sometimes elephant seal pups get separated from their mothers and need help from humans. This stranded elephant seal was rescued in Dana Point, California.

With more seals coming to the mainland, cars sometimes run into them. During their swims and dives, other things can happen. People who are fishing may hook them by accident. Or they get trapped in fishing nets

*The presence of more elephant seals has affected
other animals such as the plover.*

and cannot come up to breathe. Fortunately, these things do not happen

very often.

The increase in elephant seal numbers is affecting other animals.

The western snowy plover is a bird that is protected by law. This bird is endangered, and its population is not very large. It nests and lives in a lot of the same places where elephant seals have colonies, so the seals and the birds compete for space. Now there are large efforts to protect the seals' habitat as well as the western snowy plovers' nesting areas.

With elephant seals, there may always be new problems to solve. Fortunately, they have made a great comeback. By continuing to

Learning & Innovation Skills

Año Nuevo Point juts off the coast of central California, not far from Año Nuevo Island. Elephant seals appeared on the island in the late 1950s and started breeding there in 1961. Breeding began on the mainland in 1975. More and more seals come to the point each year to have their young. Año Nuevo now has one of the largest populations of elephant seals. Every year, more than 2,500 pups are born on the nearby islands and the mainland.

Año Nuevo is a California state reserve. A reserve is a protected place where animals can live and breed safely. All over the world, governments and ordinary citizens have set up nature reserves to protect plants and animals. What other efforts to protect the environment do you know about?

Friends of the Elephant Seal started in California in 1997. This organization of volunteers helps keep an eye on a seal colony at Piedras Blancas on California's central coast. But their main goal is to educate visitors about the seals and why it is important to protect sea life. The more they can teach people to care about elephant seals, the more "friends" the seals will have!

A healthy elephant seal bull roars on the beach at Año Nuevo State Reserve in California.

educate ourselves and others about elephant seals

and the problems they face, we can help make sure

they never will disappear.

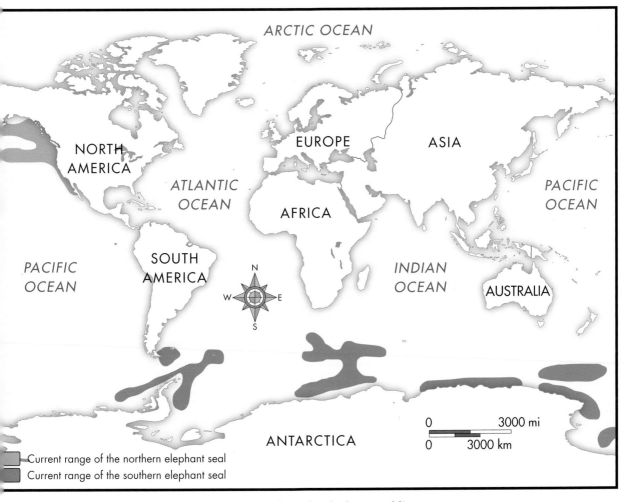

ARCTIC OCEAN

NORTH
AMERICA

EUROPE

ASIA

ATLANTIC
OCEAN

PACIFIC
OCEAN

AFRICA

SOUTH
AMERICA

PACIFIC
OCEAN

N

W   E

S

INDIAN
OCEAN

AUSTRALIA

ANTARCTICA

0   3000 mi
0   3000 km

Current range of the northern elephant seal
Current range of the southern elephant seal

This map shows where the elephant seal lives.

GLOSSARY

blubber (BLUH-bur) the thick layer of fat just under a seal or whale's skin

canines (KAY-nynz) pointed teeth that are on both sides of the mouth

carnivores (KAR-nuh-vorz) animals that eat meat

colonies (KOL-uh-neez) groups of animals that live together

dominant (DOM-uh-nuhnt) having a main or commanding position over others

endangered (en-DAYN-jurd) in danger of dying out completely

extinct (ek-STINGT) no longer living

harassed (huh-RAST) bothered or pestered

molting (MOHLT-ing) shedding the outer covering of fur, feathers, or skin so a new one can grow

phocid (FO-sid) the family of earless seals

plover (PLUHV-ur) a short-billed bird that lives by the seashore

proboscis (pruh-BAH-sis) a long, flexible snout

reserve (ri-ZURV) a protected place where animals can live and breed safely

FOR MORE INFORMATION

Books

Becker, John. *Returning Wildlife: The Northern Elephant Seal.* San Diego: KidHaven Press, 2004.

Leon, Vicki. *A Colony of Seals: The Captivating Life of a Deep Sea Diver.* Montrose, CA: London Town Press, 2005.

Rhodes, Mary Jo, and David Hall. *Dolphins, Seals, and Other Sea Mammals.* Danbury, CT: Children's Press, 2007.

Stewart, Melissa. *Seals, Sea Lions, and Walruses.* Danbury, CT: Franklin Watts, 2001.

Web Sites

Friends of the Elephant Seal
www.elephantseal.org/
For a site dedicated to educating people about elephant seals and opportunities to help them

National Geographic: Elephant Seal
www3.nationalgeographic.com/animals/mammals/elephant-seal.html
For a multimedia page including a map, sounds, and photos

INDEX

ABOUT THE AUTHOR

Susan H. Gray has a master's degree in zoology. She has written more than 70 science and reference books for children and especially loves writing about animals. Gray also likes to garden and play the piano. She lives in Cabot, Arkansas, with her husband, Michael, and many pets.